Haiku is a traditional form of Japanese poetry. Typically, a haiku is composed of three unrhymed lines of five, seven, and five syllables (for a total of just seventeen syllables). Haiku poems use strong imagery, often scenes in nature, to depict a specific moment in time or a particular emotion.

Anders Holmer is a visual artist and architect. In 2017 he wrote and illustrated his debut picture book, *Everything Happens!* (Natur & Kultur), which combined his love of both humor and poetry. He lives in Sweden.

For

Päivi

First published in the United States in 2018 by
Eerdmans Books for Young Readers,
an imprint of Wm. B. Eerdmans Publishing Co.
2140 Oak Industrial Dr. NE, Grand Rapids, Michigan 49505
www.eerdmans.com/youngreaders

Text and Illustrations © Anders Holmer and Natur & Kultur, Stockholm 2018
Published in agreement with Koja Agency
Originally published in Sweden in 2018 under the title *Regn*
English-language edition © 2018 Eerdmans Books for Young Readers

Manufactured in China

27 26 25 24 23 22 21 20 19 18   1 2 3 4 5 6 7 8 9

Library of Congress Cataloging-in-Publication Data

Names: Holmer, Anders author illustrator.
Title: Rain / written and illustrated by Anders Holmer.
Description: Grand Rapids : Eerdmans Books for Young Readers, 2018. |
   Originally published in Swedish under the title: Regn.
Identifiers: LCCN 2018005862 | ISBN 9780802855077
Subjects: LCSH: Rain—Juvenile poetry.
Classification: LCC PT9877.18.O457 A2 2018 | DDC 839.71/8—dc23 LC record available at
https://lccn.loc.gov/2018005862

Rain

Anders Holmer

Eerdmans Books for Young Readers

Grand Rapids, Michigan

The horse dreams of oats
while he is plowing the field—
crows carry off seeds.

A newspaper falls
but won't land until morning—
already old news.

Sand clouding the sun,
rustling as it lands, and a
baby tooth is loose.

Hooves thunder above
moles digging underground, and
Grandma is calling.

Slowly the boat drifts,
drifts away from the lighthouse—
never tied it up.

Beneath ashes are
seeds for a new forest that
might burn someday too.

Rain drums, train clatters—
the band joins the song, startling
swallows from their homes.

Half-awake and drenched,
a beetle stands guard in the
middle of the path.

The car radio
plays a song about the sun,
but no one hears it.

A thin metal boat
between sharp teeth and soft fur.
It's getting darker.

Calf licking the first
fresh green wedges of lichen.
And soon, butterflies!

Petals raining down,
and friends forget their quarrel—
two gentle smiles grow.